THE WIT AND WISDOM
OF SIR ALEX FERGUSON

THE
WIT AND WISDOM OF
SIR ALEX FERGUSON

COMPILED BY
CHRIS RILEY

Biteback Publishing

First published in Great Britain in 2013 by
Biteback Publishing Ltd
Westminster Tower
3 Albert Embankment
London SE1 7SP
Copyright in the selection © Chris Riley 2013

ISBN 978-184954-621-8

10 9 8 7 6 5 4 3 2 1

A CIP catalogue record for this book is available from the
British Library.

Set in Bookman and Heroic

Printed and bound in Great Britain by
CPI Group (UK) Ltd, Croydon CR0 4YY

INTRODUCTION

Sir Alex Ferguson is a true legend in the world of football. Following a career as a prolific striker in Scotland, Ferguson – or Fergie – really made his name as a manager, first at St Mirren and Aberdeen, and then, more notably, at Manchester United.

Following the sacking of Ron Atkinson, Sir Alex was appointed manager of Manchester United on 6 November 1986. At the time, Manchester United was a sleeping giant, having failed to win a league title since the glory years of Sir Matt Busby's team in the 1960s.

Despite an inauspicious start – he lost his first game 2–0 away at Oxford United – the club had great faith in Ferguson's ability and were duly rewarded when his team lifted the FA Cup in 1990, followed by the Premier League trophy three years later.

From this moment on, Ferguson's United sides would dominate English football for the next twenty years, delivering success with a regularity likely never to be repeated.

Ferguson would win a total of thirty-eight trophies while at Manchester United, in addition to the eleven he won as a manager north of the border.

Never one to shy away from controversy, Fergie has made some memorable remarks. Opposing players, managers, clubs and referees have all been on the receiving end of his acerbic tongue and this book brings together the best of his utterances, as well as some of the responses they have provoked. It also delves into his famous managerial techniques and looks at the legacy he leaves on the game.

TIMELINE

1941: Alexander Chapman Ferguson is born on 31 December in Govan, Glasgow.

1957: Makes his playing debut as a sixteen-year-old amateur for Queen's Park.

1960: Despite averaging just below a goal a game, Ferguson can't hold down a regular starting place, and moves to St Johnstone.

1964: Ferguson continues to score goals on a regular basis but again finds himself out of the team and moves to Dunfermline, becoming a full-time professional footballer.

1967: An impressive record of sixty-six goals in just eighty-nine games convinces Rangers to part company with £65,000 to secure his services, then a record fee for a transfer between two Scottish clubs.

1974: Retires as a player at the age of thirty-two and is appointed manager of East Stirlingshire. However, he leaves this role in October to move to St Mirren after taking advice from legendary manager Jock Stein.

1977: Wins his first trophy as a manager as his St Mirren team are crowned First Division champions.

1978: Appointed Aberdeen manager.

1980: Aberdeen are crowned Scottish champions, the first time in fifteen years the league has not been won by either Celtic or Rangers, and Aberdeen's first title since 1955.

1983: Wins his first European trophy as Aberdeen defeat Real Madrid in the final of the European Cup Winners' Cup. Ferguson is awarded an OBE.

1985: Takes over as Scotland manager after the sudden death of mentor Jock Stein but leaves the post the following year.

1986: Ferguson's success in Scotland attracts the attention of Manchester United, who appoint him manager following the sacking of Ron Atkinson.

1990: Wins his first trophy, the FA Cup, as United manager. His side beat Crystal Palace 1–0 in a replay.

1993: United win their first title since 1967 and follow it by winning the league and cup double the subsequent year.

1995: Ferguson is awarded a CBE.

1999: Arguably Sir Alex's greatest year. Manchester United complete the treble by winning the Premier League, the FA Cup and the Champions League, United's first European triumph since Sir Matt Busby's iconic side of 1968. They finish the year as world champions after defeating Brazilian side Palmeiras 1–0 in the final of the Intercontinental Cup. Ferguson is knighted.

2001: Ferguson announces his intention to retire following the 2001/2 season; however, he signs a new contract the following February.

2004: Wins his fifth and final FA Cup, a record in the modern era.

2008: Manchester United become European champions for the second time under Ferguson's guidance, defeating Chelsea 6–5 on penalties after a 1–1 draw.

2010: Overtakes Sir Matt Busby as Manchester United's longest-serving manager.

2011: United beat Chelsea into second place to record their nineteenth league title, surpassing Liverpool's eighteen and knocking them off their perch in the process.

2013: Announces his retirement as manager of Manchester United after 1,500 matches and twenty-six years in charge, winning thirty-eight trophies in the process. Sir Alex announces he will continue at the club as a director and ambassador.

MANAGERIAL HONOURS

St Mirren
Scottish First Division (1):1976/7

Aberdeen
Scottish Premier Division (3): 1979/80, 1983/4, 1984/5
Scottish Cup (4): 1981/2, 1982/3, 1983/4, 1985/6
Scottish League Cup (1): 1985/6
UEFA Cup Winners' Cup (1): 1982/3
UEFA Super Cup (1): 1983

Manchester United
Premier League (13): 1992/3, 1993/4, 1995/6, 1996/7,
    1998/9, 1999/2000, 2000/2001, 2002/3, 2006/7,
    2007/8, 2008/9, 2010/11, 2012/13
FA Cup (5): 1989/90, 1993/4, 1995/6, 1998/9, 2003/4
League Cup (4): 1991/2, 2005/6, 2008/9, 2009/10
FA Charity/Community Shield (10): 1990 (shared with
    Liverpool), 1993, 1994, 1996, 1997, 2003, 2007,
    2008, 2010, 2011
UEFA Champions League (2): 1998/9, 2007/8
UEFA Cup Winners' Cup (1): 1990/1
UEFA Super Cup (1): 1991
Intercontinental Cup (1): 1999
FIFA Club World Cup (1): 2008

"I can't believe it. I can't believe it. Football. Bloody hell!"

In the aftermath of Manchester United's dramatic win in the 1999 Champions League Final. His side scored two goals in injury time to beat Bayern Munich 2–1 and win the world's premier club competition for the first time in thirty-one years.

"The players couldn't pick each other out. They said it was difficult to see their team-mates at distance when they lifted their heads. It was nothing to do with superstition. This club went twenty-six years without winning the league and we didn't think about changing the red shirts. It's nothing to do with that at all."

Ferguson's famous excuse for Manchester United's terrible performance in the first half of a match against relegation favourites Southampton in 1996. Losing 3–0 at half-time, United changed into their blue-and-white third strip for the second half. They lost the game 3–1, and the kit was never worn again.

"I can't understand the Leeds players. I'm absolutely in support of their manager [Howard Wilkinson]. He doesn't deserve his players. If they had played like that all season they'd be near the top. They raised their game because they were playing Manchester United. It was pathetic. I think we can accept any club coming here and trying their hardest, so long as they do it every week."

Accusing the Leeds United side of trying harder than usual in a match against Manchester United in 1996. Newcastle United manager Kevin Keegan was so outraged by Ferguson's comment that he launched into the now infamous 'I'd love it' rant. Ferguson's side overhauled Newcastle's twelve-point lead, and eventually won the league by four points.

"My greatest challenge is not what is happening right at this moment, my greatest challenge was knocking Liverpool right off their fucking perch. And you can print that."

Following his appointment at Manchester United in 1986 Liverpool would only win two more league titles, and have won none since United's first under Ferguson.

"It was a freakish incident. If I'd tried it a hundred times or a million times, it wouldn't happen again. If it did, I would carry on playing."

On the flying boot hitting David Beckham in the face. Manchester United had just crashed out of the FA Cup at home to Arsenal when Ferguson kicked a stray boot in frustration across the dressing room. Beckham left Manchester United for Real Madrid at the end of the season.

"It's getting tickly now – squeaky-bum time, I call it."

Perhaps Ferguson's most memorable remark, uttered during the closely fought title race with Arsenal in 2003. Ferguson's side reeled in the eight-point lead Arsenal held at the beginning of March to win the league by five points.

'Squeaky-bum time' was added to the Collins English Dictionary *in 2005 and defined as 'the tense final stages of a league competition, especially from the point of view of the leaders'.*

"Sometimes you look in a field and you see a cow and you think it's a better cow than the one you've got in your own field. It's a fact. Right? And it never really works out that way."

Trying his best to explain to the media the nature of Wayne Rooney's request to leave Manchester United in 2010. Whatever Ferguson said to Rooney, it worked, as the striker signed a new contract with the club just days later.

"When an Italian tells me it's pasta on the plate, I check under the sauce to make sure. They are the inventors of the smokescreen."

Ferguson takes a diplomatic stance prior to a Champions League quarter-final tie against Inter Milan in 1999.

"They come out with 'the English are so strong, we're terrible in the air, we can't do this, we can't do that'. Then they beat you 3–0."

On Italians.

"It can be difficult to pinpoint who would make it as a manager. For instance, nobody here thought Mark Hughes would become a manager, never in a million years, and we all thought Bryan Robson was a certainty to be a top manager."

Explaining that his judgement hasn't always been correct. Former captain Bryan Robson would go on to have relatively short managerial stints at Bradford City and West Brom among others, while Mark Hughes has managed four Premier League teams as well as the Welsh national side.

"There is no doubt about it. They were never getting through that tie; with eleven men we had no problem. The young boy showed a bit of inexperience but they got him sent off. Everyone sprinted towards the referee – typical Germans."

Doing his bit for international relations. Ferguson was unhappy at the conduct of the Bayern Munich players and accused them of persuading the referee to send off Rafael da Silva during a Champions League quarter-final tie in 2010.

"You must be joking. Do I look as if I'm a masochist ready to cut myself? How does relegation sound instead?"

After being asked if rivals Liverpool were good enough to mount a title challenge in 2007.

"Look at me – it's taken ten years off me today. It's these tablets, they're great!"

Following Manchester United's 3–0 victory over Aston Villa, securing them a record twentieth league title and Ferguson his thirteenth.

"At the end of this game, the European Cup will be only six feet away from you, and you'll not even be able to touch it if we lose. And for many of you, that will be the closest you will ever get. Don't you dare come back in here without giving your all."

Arguably the most important half-time team talk of Ferguson's career, delivered with United losing 1–0 to Bayern Munich in the 1999 Champions League Final. United went on to win 2–1 with two goals in injury time, and become European champions for the first time since 1968.

"I'm no' wanting that on. I want to cancel that interview right? The whole fucking lot of it. Cancel it. You know the fucking score, son, so fucking make sure that it doesn't go out or you'll never get in this fucking club again."

Even legendary commentator John Motson was on the receiving end of a blast from the 'hairdryer' after asking if Ferguson's captain Roy Keane would be disciplined by the club following another red card.

"I'm not saying what they do down there, but next year we'll be sending somebody to see how it happens, I can assure you. I just don't understand how you can get the fixtures like that."

On the fixture list generated at random by an FA computer.

"It would have been Sir Matt Busby's ninetieth birthday today, but I think he was up there doing a lot of kicking."

After United's victory in the 1999 Champions League Final.

"They have those fans who are so emotional and fanatical they expect to win the World Cup."

On the fervent support enjoyed by rivals Newcastle United.

"He'll be getting a hug and a kiss from me – maybe even two!"

On fellow manager Sam Allardyce after his Bolton Wanderers side drew 2–2 with Chelsea, United's rivals for the title, in 2007.

"The press have had a field day out of it. They have addressed every possible avenue. The only one they have left out is Barack Obama. He is too busy."

On the press coverage of his argument with Newcastle United manager Alan Pardew.

"If we can play like that every week we'll get some level of consistency."

On, erm, consistency.

"I tell the players that the bus is moving. This club has to progress. And the bus wouldn't wait for them. I tell them to get on board."

Revealing how he motivates his players.

"The crowd were dead. It was like a funeral out there."

On a rather subdued atmosphere at Old Trafford.

"If Chelsea drop points, the cat's out in the open. And you know what cats are like – sometimes they don't come home."

Questioning the ability of rivals Chelsea to hold on to their lead in the Premier League title race.

"It is totally out of the question. There is no way we would sell him, or any of our best players."

On the rumours circulating in the media that Manchester United would be selling David Beckham. Two months later, Beckham was sold to Real Madrid.

"Cole should be scoring from those distances, but I'm not going to single him out."

Unsuccessfully attempting to avoid singling out the poor performance of striker Andy Cole.

"On you go. I'm no' fucking talking to you. He's a fucking great player. Youse are fucking idiots."

After being asked one question too many about the poor form of £28 million signing Juan Sebastián Verón. The midfielder was sold after just two seasons at Manchester United.

"I don't give any of you credibility. You talk about wanting to have an association with people here and you wonder why I don't get on with you? But you're a fucking embarrassment. One of these days the door is going to be shut on you permanently."

During a particularly low point in his relationship with the media.

"Myths grow all the time. If I was to listen to the number of times I've thrown teacups then we've gone through some crockery in this place."

On the rumours surrounding his short temper in the dressing room and his tendency to throw teacups.

"We have people coming here to admire the scenery and enjoy their crisps."

Ferguson questions the support of the crowd at Old Trafford.

"Struggling? Are you serious? We're not struggling."

Following a disappointing result against Benfica in the group stages of the Champions League, 2011. United were subsequently knocked out of the competition the following game.

"You're a fucking bottler, Incey! You cannae handle the stage, can you? You are a fucking bottler!"

Paul Ince receives the 'hairdryer treatment' at half-time during a match against Barcelona in the group stages of the Champions League, 1994.

"I'm going to tell you the story about the geese which fly 5,000 miles from Canada to France. They fly in V-formation but the second ones don't fly. They're the subs for the first ones. And then the second ones take over – so it's teamwork."

Ferguson articulates the importance of teamwork in unique fashion.

"He nearly killed me. He forgets I'm seventy-one."

On Robin van Persie. The striker gave his manager a bear hug after ending a ten-match goal drought.

"That's absolute bollocks, that. Absolute nonsense."

When asked if a week in which his team had suffered two defeats in a row was the most difficult of his career.

"That's one of the most stupid questions I've ever heard in my life."

After being asked which Barcelona player he would choose to sign if given a blank cheque. The Barcelona team contained four-time World Player of the Year Lionel Messi.

"It keeps those fuckers from the media out."

On Manchester United's newly built training complex, known as 'Fortress Carrington'.

"As with every young player, he's only eighteen."

On a youthful David Beckham.

"Only true champions come out and show their worth after defeat – and I expect us to do that."

Making his expectations of his team clear in 2006.

"We're the luckiest team in the world. We were a disgrace of a performance. [Willie] Miller and [Alex] McLeish won the cup for Aberdeen. Miller and McLeish played Rangers themselves. They were a disgrace of a performance. And I'm no' caring, winning cups doesn't matter. Our standards have been set long ago and we're not going to accept that from any Aberdeen team. No way should we take any glory from that."

Moments after his Aberdeen side had retained the Scottish Cup with a 1–0 victory over Rangers in the final, 1983.

"What the fuck are you lot playing at? That is the biggest load of shite I've ever seen. Not one of you can look me in the eye, because not one of you deserves to have a say. I can't believe you've come here and decided to toss it off like that crap you're playing out there."

Subjecting his players to the 'hairdryer' at half-time during a match against Sheffield Wednesday in 1998.

"It was particularly pleasing that our goal-scorers scored tonight."

On scoring goals.

"The philosophy of a lot of European teams, even in home matches, is not to give a goal away."

Pinpointing exactly why European sides have had so much success.

"I bet him he wouldn't get fifteen league goals and I'm going to have to change my bet with him. If he gets to fifteen I can change it and I am allowed to do that because I'm the manager. I'm going to make it 150 now!"

On an ill-advised bet with star winger Cristiano Ronaldo.

"This pilot move by FIFA will take root and fly."

On a programme initiated by the game's rulers that Ferguson was, presumably, hoping would take off.

"The lads ran their socks into the ground."

Ferguson has always asked for more from his players than any other manager.

"We're suffering because of what happened against Arsenal ... One of my players would have to be hit by an axe to get a penalty at the moment."

Ferguson questions the recent performances of referees in Manchester United's matches.

"This was an important day and we wanted everyone together. In that situation, it was best to leave Ruud out."

On the dropping of star striker Ruud van Nistelrooy.

"It's a really proud moment for me. Normally people die before they have a statue. I'm outliving death!"

On the unveiling of his statue outside Old Trafford.

"I can still remember my very first game in charge away at Oxford. I had done my team talk and was going into the dugout when I saw the bus driver sitting there. He was even giving the tea out at half-time. Let's say that quickly stopped."

On the level of professionalism at United when he took over in 1986.

"I think they're responsible for their actions, responsible for what they say on their Twitter. I don't understand it, to be honest with you ... There's a billion things you could do with your life. You could go to the library and read a book."

On players using Twitter, after a controversial outburst from Wayne Rooney.

"You've been told not to fucking ask that – right? Cut that off, cut that off [pointing to tape recorder]. Fucking idiots, you all are. You do that again and you won't be coming back here. You fucking sell your papers and radio shows on the back of this club."

When asked a question on the future of David Beckham.

"They did a story about my son that was a whole lot of nonsense. It was a horrible attack on my son's honour and he should never have been accused of that. I think the BBC is the kind of company that never apologise and they never will apologise. They are arrogant beyond belief."

On his seven-year boycott of BBC journalists.

"Gary Lineker – a bright boy from the BBC – says I'm childish. Well, he should know about that himself. He's been subjected to a lot of stuff in the media himself and he's had stuff stopped from getting in newspapers from time to time. So he'll understand what childishness means, because he is childish. I don't think I'm childish at all."

On Gary Lineker, after the Match of the Day *presenter described Sir Alex as 'childish' for refusing to speak to the BBC.*

ON PLAYERS

During a managerial career spanning five decades, Ferguson has come across thousands of players – and hasn't looked upon all of them favourably.

"Would Kenny have signed for Blackburn when he was a player? I know what he would have done if United and Blackburn had both come in for him."

On striker Alan Shearer's decision to sign for Kenny Dalglish's Blackburn Rovers rather than Manchester United in 1992. Blackburn would go on to win the Premier League in 1995, Shearer's only league title.

"He was blessed with great stamina, the best of all the players I've had here. After training, he'd always be practising, practising, practising. But his life changed when he met his wife. She's in pop and David got another image. He's developed this 'fashion thing' – I saw his transition to a different person."

On the transformation of David Beckham into an international superstar. The breakdown in their relationship led to Beckham moving to Real Madrid in 2003.

"He was thirteen and just floated over the ground like a cocker spaniel chasing a piece of silver paper in the wind."

Describing the first time he saw winger Ryan Giggs play. Under Ferguson's management, Giggs has gone on to become the most decorated player in English football history.

"If he tries to bully you he will fucking enjoy it. Don't ever let him bully you. Right? You just make sure you are ready for him. That's all you need to worry about. He's a fucking big-time Charlie."

Referring to former player and then Liverpool midfielder Paul Ince in a team talk prior to United's match against Liverpool in 1998.

"After attending the press conference, I started to get the jitters about the whole business. Not quite panic, but uncertainty as to whether we had done the right thing. I began worrying about all the controversial stuff being traded around about Eric's past."

On the signing of controversial forward Eric Cantona from rivals Leeds United in 1992. United fans later voted for Cantona as the club's greatest ever player.

"Here he is, the boy who's given me all this grey hair!"

Referring to treble-winning striker Dwight Yorke.

"If he was an inch taller he'd be the best centre-half in Britain. His father is six-foot two – I'd check the milkman."

Questioning the identity of long-serving right-back Gary Neville's father.

"That lad must have been born offside."

On Italian striker and goalhanger extraordinaire
Filippo Inzaghi.

"I used to have a saying that when a player is at his peak, he feels as though he can climb Everest in his slippers. That's what he was like."

On star midfielder Paul Ince.

"He was towering over me and the other players were almost covering their eyes. I'm looking up and thinking, 'If he does hit me, I'm dead.'"

Referring to a half-time argument with 6ft 3in goalkeeper Peter Schmeichel.

"Ryan Giggs is a freak – a unique freak."

As opposed to a run-of-the-mill freak.

"I don't think I could have a higher opinion of any footballer than I already had of the Irishman, but he rose even further in my estimation at the Stadio Delle Alpi. The minute he was booked and out of the final he seemed to redouble his efforts to get the team there. It was the most emphatic display of selflessness I have seen on a football field. Pounding over every blade of grass, competing as if he would rather die of exhaustion than lose, he inspired all around him. I felt such an honour to be associated with such a player."

On Roy Keane's performance against Juventus in the second leg of the Champions League semi-final in 1999. Having been booked, Keane was suspended from the final against Bayern Munich. He received a medal but famously said it was worth nothing as he had not played in the winning game.

"It was one of the mistakes I made – hopefully I haven't made too many – but that was one. I got this offer from Lazio for £18.5 million. Was it £18.5 million? No, £16.5 million I think it was, and I says, 'Can't turn it down. He's thirty years of age.' I thought if we could get Laurent Blanc for a year or so and bring the young ones through – like Wes Brown and John O'Shea – but it backfired."

On treble-winning centre-back Jaap Stam, sold to Lazio after angering Ferguson with revelations in his autobiography. Stam won three Premier League titles in his three seasons at Old Trafford. United would only win one more in the five years after his departure.

"Can you fucking believe him?"

On seeing goalkeeper Peter Schmeichel going up for a corner in the 1999 Champions League Final. United subsequently equalised and went on to win in the most dramatic fashion.

"He could start a row in an empty house."

On ultra-aggressive Chelsea midfielder Dennis Wise.

"Suárez is a disgrace to Liverpool Football Club. He should not be allowed to play for Liverpool again. He could have caused a riot."

On controversial Liverpool striker Luis Suárez following his refusal to shake the hand of United defender Patrice Evra before a game.

"Whether dribbling or sprinting, Ryan can leave the best defenders with twistcd blood."

On Ryan Giggs's control over a football.

"If ever there was one player, anywhere in the world, that was made for Manchester United, it was Cantona. He swaggered in, stuck his chest out, raised his head and surveyed everything as though he were asking: 'I'm Cantona. How big are you? Are you big enough for me?'"

On cult hero Eric 'The King' Cantona, one of Ferguson's most successful signings.

ON OPPOSING MANAGERS

Ferguson has had tempestuous relationships with many rival managers during his career. Here he gives his views on a few of those who have occupied the opposition dugout.

"I read that Scolari is more experienced than me. What have I been doing for the last thirty-four years? I must have missed something or been asleep somewhere. They are saying because of Scolari's experience, Chelsea are going to win the league. I don't understand that."

Questioning the credentials of Luiz Felipe Scolari, the new manager of rivals Chelsea, in 2008.

"In the tunnel Wenger was criticising my players, calling them cheats, so I told him to leave them alone and behave himself. To not apologise for the behaviour of the players to another manager is unthinkable. It's a disgrace, but I don't expect Wenger to ever apologise, he's that type of person."

On Arsène Wenger, following the fight between Manchester United and Arsenal players, dubbed 'Pizzagate' after Arsenal midfielder Cesc Fàbregas allegedly threw a slice of pizza at the United manager in 2004.

"I think he was an angry man. He must have been disturbed for some reason. I think you have got to cut through the venom of it and hopefully he'll reflect and understand what he said was absolutely ridiculous."

Following Liverpool manager Rafael Benítez's rant at Manchester United and Ferguson in 2009.

"They say he's an intelligent man, right? Speaks five languages? I've got a fifteen-year-old boy from the Ivory Coast who speaks five languages."

Ferguson raises his doubts about the appointment of Arsène Wenger as Arsenal manager, 1996.

"He was certainly full of it, calling me 'Boss' and 'Big Man' when we had our post-match drink after the first leg, but it would help if his greetings were accompanied by a decent glass of wine. What he gave me was paint stripper."

On his first meeting with future Chelsea manager José Mourinho, then manager of Porto.

"Wenger doesn't know anything about English football. He's at a big club – well, Arsenal used to be big. He should keep his mouth shut, firmly shut ... He's a novice – he should keep his opinions to Japanese football."

On Arsène Wenger shortly after his move to England from Japanese club Nagoya Grampus Eight in 1996. Wenger's Arsenal side would go on to win three Premier League titles and four FA Cups in the following years.

"I remember his first press conference
[at Chelsea, in 2004] and I thought: 'Christ,
he's a cocky bastard, him.' He was telling
the players: 'Look, I'm the special one, we
don't lose games.'"

*Recalling José Mourinho's memorable entrance into
English football.*

"I think he is very concerned about his CV.
He refers to it quite a lot."

*On rival Rafael Benítez's preoccupation with his record of
achievements.*

"Rafa Benítez is very lucky because on his CV in two weeks' time he could have two World Championships to his name – and nothing to do with the teams. José Mourinho won the treble after going to Inter Milan. He [Benítez] took over and won a World Championship without having to do anything. He had nothing to do with the construction of the teams and that's where I feel real disappointment for Roberto Di Matteo. He could really have on his CV an FA Cup, a Champions League and a World Club Championship."

Ferguson makes plain his view that rival Rafael Benítez may be receiving more credit than he deserves after winning the World Club Championship with Inter Milan (prior to losing another final with Chelsea).

"I remember a few years ago when Liverpool beat us 4–1 at Old Trafford. That genius [Rafael] Benítez said they had planned to beat us by playing long balls behind us. Remember that? Clown."

On the tactics of Rafael Benítez.

"We will only be in trouble if we listen to José too much."

On outspoken rival José Mourinho.

"He refereed the game. He was out on that touchline the whole game haranguing the referee, the fourth official and the linesmen. The minute I come off the bench for a bad tackle by de Jong on Welbeck, he was out again. He can't have it both ways. He's been complaining about referees this season but he won't be complaining tonight that's for sure."

On Manchester City manager Roberto Mancini.

ON RIVAL CLUBS

Ferguson has seen many rivals to United's supremacy come and go during his career. Here are some of his more controversial observations.

"Do you think I would enter into a contract with that mob? Absolutely no chance. I would not sell them a virus. That is a 'No' by the way. There is no agreement whatsoever between the clubs."

On the rumours linking Cristiano Ronaldo to Real Madrid in December 2008. Six months later, Ronaldo was sold to Real Madrid for a world record £80 million.

"It's City, isn't it? They are a small club, with a small mentality. All they can talk about is Manchester United, that's all they've done and they can't get away from it. They think taking Tévez away from Manchester United is a triumph. It is poor stuff."

Heating up the Manchester rivalry in 2009, referring to the 'Welcome to Manchester' poster featuring former United striker Carlos Tévez.

"Sometimes you have a noisy neighbour. You cannot do anything about that. They will always be noisy. You just have to get on with your life, put your television on and turn it up a bit louder."

Attempting to put rivals Manchester City in their place in 2009.

"You get used to this, Madrid's behaviour on these things. I read about [Real's President Ramón] Calderón making the great statement that slavery was abolished many, many years ago. Well, did they tell Franco that? Jesus Christ! Eh, give me a break!"

On Real Madrid's attempts to sign Manchester United star Cristiano Ronaldo in 2008.

"Our rich history stands us aside – it's better than anyone. It would take City a century to get our level of history."

Laying down the gauntlet to 'noisy neighbours' Manchester City.

"What made it really obscene was that Madrid, as General Franco's club, had a history of being able to get whoever and whatever they wanted before democracy came to Spain."

Ferguson proffers the controversial theory that Real Madrid's behaviour in their pursuit of Cristiano Ronaldo may be based on their historic links with former Spanish dictator General Franco.

"I carry that because I am the manager of the most famous club in the world. I am not like Newcastle, a wee club in the north-east."

Ferguson doesn't hold back during a public spat with Newcastle manager Alan Pardew.

ON REFEREES

With a short temper, Ferguson has often been highly critical of the performance of referees in the immediate aftermath of a match, particularly if his side have lost.

"The pace of the game demanded a referee who was fit. It is an indictment of our game. You see referees abroad who are as fit as butchers' dogs. We have some who are fit. He wasn't fit. He was taking thirty seconds to book a player. He was needing a rest. It was ridiculous."

Unhappy at the performance, or lack thereof, of referee Alan Wiley following Manchester United's draw with Sunderland in 2009. This outburst earned Ferguson a four-match touchline ban and a £20,000 fine from the FA.

"You can't applaud a referee."

Making his views on referees clear.

"All I do is point at my watch to help the referee make the right decisions."

On his famous timekeeping ability and 'pointing-to-watch' gesture.

"You want a fair referee – or a strong referee anyway – and we didn't get that. I must say, when I saw who the referee was I feared it. I feared the worst."

Ferguson gives his views on the appointment of referee Martin Atkinson for Manchester United's match at Chelsea in 2011. Ferguson's comments earned him a five-match touchline ban and a £30,000 fine.

"Can anyone tell me why they give referees a watch? It's certainly not for keeping the time."

Ferguson yet again questions the ability of referees to keep an eye on their watches.

"I think everyone who watched the game agreed [the red card was unjust]. I think [former referee] Dermot Gallagher said it was the worst decision of the week. Everyone knows it was a bad decision, but it happens. Unfortunately, in a game of that magnitude, it could have had a big impact. It didn't help us in terms of trying to go and win the game."

Explaining that having a man sent off was not going to be of benefit to his team after Nani's controversial red card in United's 2013 Champions League quarter-final against Real Madrid.

"They gave us four minutes [injury time], that's an insult to the game. It denies you a proper chance to win a football match. That's obvious to everyone today and it's a flaw in the game that the referee is responsible for timekeeping. It's ridiculous that it's 2012 and the referee still has control of that."

Complaining about the lack of 'Fergie time' after a loss to Tottenham.

WHAT THEY SAY

Ferguson's comments and methods have outraged many a managerial rival throughout his career. Here we look at what they have to say about him.

"You have the rules, or not the rules. You observe the rules, or not the rules. Why should anyone be scared of Ferguson? I don't understand that."

Arsène Wenger

"It's exactly what Arsène Wenger was saying one day. When we were rivals, we were no longer friends. When we were twenty points behind Manchester United, he liked me."

Rafael Benítez

"I think it's the money they were spending. If you analyse the transfer record and the history ... [Wayne] Rooney, or [Rio] Ferdinand, for example ... £30 million for a young player or a centre-back. Every year they [United] are very well off. It's not just because of the interviews or the press conferences; it's because they had money."

Rafael Benítez, after being asked whether he thought Ferguson's personality was behind Manchester United's success.

"I was waiting – I was waiting at the beginning [of the match]. It's his decision. I was ready and waiting [to shake], I have some education. I was waiting, I have education because I know that a lot of people are watching so I know what I have to do."

Rafael Benítez, on Ferguson's refusal to shake hands with him after a game.

"Him? No. He doesn't talk with the referee or the fourth official? No, never."

Roberto Mancini responds sarcastically after Ferguson accused him of 'badgering' the referee.

"During the Respect campaign – and this is a fact – Mr Ferguson was charged by the FA for improper conduct after comments made about Martin Atkinson and Keith Hackett. He was not punished. He is the only manager in the league that cannot be punished for these things.

Then he was talking about the fixtures. Two years ago we were playing a lot of early kick-offs away on Saturdays when United were playing on Sundays. And we didn't say anything. Now he is complaining about everything, that everybody is against United.

We had a meeting in Manchester with managers and the FA about the Respect campaign. And I was very clear: forget the campaign because Mr Ferguson was killing the referees, killing Mr Atkinson, killing Mr Hackett. But he is not punished. How can you talk about the Respect campaign and criticise the referee every single week?

All managers need to know is that only Mr Ferguson can talk about the fixtures, can talk about referees and nothing happens."

Rafael Benítez, during his infamous rant in 2009.

"I've kept really quiet but I'll tell you something, he went down in my estimation when he said that. We have not resorted to that. You can tell him now, we're still fighting for this title and he's got to go to Middlesbrough and get something. And I'll tell you, honestly, I will love it if we beat them. Love it."

Kevin Keegan's infamous 'I would love it' rant, aimed at Ferguson during the title run-in to the 1995/6 season, following Fergie's assertion that teams try harder when playing Manchester United.

"A lot of officials would be in awe of him and afraid to upset him. I never had any doubts about that. If there was a bit of time to be added they would make sure they got it right because they did not want to upset him. Especially young referees, and even one or two of the older ones, were a little bit afraid to upset him."

Harry Redknapp.

ON RETIREMENT

Despite first announcing that he would retire at the end of the 2001/2 season, Ferguson continued as Manchester United manager for another eleven years. However, he flirted with the idea on a number of occasions after deciding to carry on.

"I will be leaving Manchester United at the end of the season and that is it."

Announcing his retirement from the game in 2002.

"It was really Cathy's [his wife's] idea. If she hadn't come up with it and the boys [sons Mark, Darren and Jason] hadn't given full support, I wouldn't have considered a change of mind. But I do have to confess that maybe it was an idea I was hoping deep down that she would come up with."

On his subsequent change of heart about retirement, later in 2002.

"There obviously will be a point when I do quit and when it is I absolutely have no idea because I tried that, and it was an absolute disaster. [I was in] agony, absolute agony [at the thought of retiring]. My wife made me change my mind and she was dead right. I think she thought she would soon be fed up with me around the house."

Ferguson hinting that he may have been encouraged to scrap his retirement plans in 2002.

"I'm pleased to be staying – but once this contract is up, that will be it. I have no intention of staying on at the club in any capacity whatsoever."

Referring to his new contract, ending in 2005.

"I still have a lot of passion. I'm still happy. But I'm sixty-six now – maybe three years more, then I'll finish."

More retirement talk, this time in 2007.

"I won't be doing a Bobby Robson and be a manager when I am seventy. It is just knowing when to quit. Football is like a drug which is difficult to give up."

Speaking in 2008. Ferguson would eventually retire at the age of seventy-one.

"I am such a bloody talented guy. I might go into painting or something like that."

On his plans for retirement.

SECRETS OF MANAGEMENT

Ferguson's management skills are renowned the world over, and it has been said that he would have been a success in whatever field he had chosen to pursue. Here he gives advice on motivation and discipline.

On player power:

"Some English clubs have changed managers so many times that it creates power for the players in the dressing room. That is very dangerous. Football management in the end is all about the players. You think you are a better player than they are, and they think they are a better manager than you are."

On giving a memorable team talk:

"I once heard a coach start with: 'This must be the thousandth team talk I've had with you,' and saw a player respond with: 'Yeah, and I've slept through half of them.' So I tell different stories and use my imagination."

On using the 'hairdryer':

"There is no room for criticism on the training field. For a player – and for any human being – there is nothing better than hearing 'well done'. Those are the two best words ever invented in sports. Also, you can't always come in [after a game] shouting and screaming. That doesn't work."

On forward thinking:

"In the dressing room, it's necessary that you point out your players' mistakes. I do it right after the game. I don't wait until Monday, I do it, and it's finished. I'm on to the next match. There is no point in criticising a player forever."

On criticism:

"No one likes to get criticised ... I never discuss an individual player in public. The players know that. It stays indoors."

On dealing with superstar players:

"We fine them, but we keep it indoors. You can't ever lose control – not when you are dealing with thirty top professionals who are all millionaires. And if anyone steps out of my control, that's them dead."

On the importance of building a club:

"The first thought for 99 per cent of new managers is to make sure they win – to survive. They bring experienced players in, often from their previous clubs. But I think it is important to build a structure for a football club, not just a football team. You need a foundation. And there is nothing better than seeing a young player make it to the first team. The idea is that the younger players are developing and meeting the standards that the older ones have set before."

On aggression:

"One of my players has been sent off several times. He will do something if he gets the chance – even in training. Can I take it out of him? No. Would I want to take it out of him? No. If you take the aggression out of him, he is not himself. So you have to accept that there is a certain flaw that is counter-balanced by all the great things he can do."

On hard work:

"I tell players that hard work is a talent, too. They need to work harder than anyone else. And if they can no longer bring the discipline that we ask for here at United, they are out. I am only interested in players who really want to play for United, and who, like me, are bad losers."

On dropping players:

"I do it privately. It's not easy, but I do them all myself. It is important. I have been dropped from a cup final in Scotland as a player at ten past two, so I know what it feels like. I'm not ever sure what they are thinking, but I tend to say: 'Look, I might be making a mistake here,' – I always say that – 'but I think this is the best team for today.'"

On repetition and discipline:

"Some managers are 'pleasing managers'. They let the players play eight-a-sides – games they enjoy. But here, we look at the training sessions as opportunities to learn and improve. Sometimes the players may think 'here we go again', but it helps to win. The message is simple: we cannot sit still at this club."

On his history as a player:

"Do you think Rooney cares? He'll laugh at me and say: 'Boss, it was so long ago, and in Scotland. Are they still part-timers up there?'"

On changing with the times:

"Players live more sheltered lives. They are more fragile than twenty-five years ago. I used to be very aggressive. I am still very passionate and want to win but I have mellowed. Age does that to you."

On dealing with disappointment:

"Another day in the history of Manchester United, that's all it was [when rivals City won the Premier League]. It created the drama that only United can produce. I've still got a wee bit of anger in me, thinking of how we threw the league away last season. My motivation to the players will be that we can't let City beat us twice in a row."

On his traditional post-match drink with opposing managers:

"You have to get the game out of your system quickly or it becomes an obsession. Win, lose or draw. We show our face and keep our dignity. We are Manchester United."

On not becoming preoccupied by the opposition:

"Tactics can change depending on whom we are playing. I tend to concentrate on one or two players of my opponents – the ones that are the most influential. Who's the guy who is taking all the free kicks? Who's the guy who's on the ball all the time? Who's the one urging everyone on? The rest of the time I concentrate on our own team."

On his winning mentality:

"I've never played for a draw in my life."

On superstars:

"The work of a team should always embrace a great player but the great player must always work."

On modesty:

"Part of my job is to make sure these lads keep their feet on the ground. I hammer it into them that the work ethic is what got them through the door here in the first place and they must never lose it. I say to them, 'When you go home to your mother, make sure she is seeing the same person she sent to me, because if you take all this fame and money the wrong way, your mother'll be disappointed with you.'"

On his high standards:

"I never give in or give up easily on either a player or a cause. Even if the team have won, I'm not always happy because standards are all-important to me and, if they have dropped, I'm angry."

On never giving up:

"As long as there are games to play it is not over."

THE LEGACY OF SIR ALEX

Sir Alex Ferguson goes down as one of the most successful managers in history and retires in 2013 widely respected by the footballing world. Here, rivals, players and football luminaries pay tribute.

"He's unique, especially in the modern day. If you go back many years then you will find somebody like him, but [it's amazing] in the modern day at the highest level, where it is really difficult to survive in our job. He's absolutely incredible at what he does."

"I don't call him Sir, Mister, Alex or Ferguson. I call him Boss."

José Mourinho, former Chelsea manager and rival.

"In my eyes he's the best manager of all time."

Wayne Rooney, one of Ferguson's most expensive purchases at Manchester United.

"He gave me the freedom I needed on the pitch. I found the perfect manager and the perfect club."

Eric Cantona, former Manchester United captain.

"I don't know anybody who has done twenty-five years at the top level with the same club. It is exceptional. Certainly nobody will do it again."

Arsène Wenger, Arsenal manager and long-time rival.

"In 2005/6 we thought Chelsea had changed the face of English football forever ... And then Manchester City last year, I thought ... it's gone, Man United will struggle to come back. Of course, the very next season they win the title at a canter. And that's Alex Ferguson for you."

Alan Hansen, former Liverpool defender.

"He's got to be the best club manager there's ever been. It's unbelievable to change around four different squads to have the success that he's had, and rebuild a team like that. That is real good management. You don't really think of him as Sir Alex, it's always been 'The Boss'."

Bryan Robson, former Manchester United captain.

"I think he's been the greatest British manager in football history … and quite possibly in the world. Phenomenally successful."

Gary Lineker, former England striker.

"His know-how, his desire, his hunger, his will to win and longevity are absolutely staggering. He's an absolute genius. If you could bottle that, it'd be worth a fortune."

Alan Shearer, former England striker.

"The amount of success he's had will never be repeated. And it's also been achieved ... with a lot of style. His teams have always played well, which is the Old Trafford way, it's the Manchester United way."

Ron Atkinson, Ferguson's predecessor as Manchester United manager.

"He has been the greatest manager the game has ever known, there's no question about that."

Jimmy Greaves, former England striker.

"Sir Alex has made a massive contribution to football, not only in Scotland and in England, but across Europe and beyond. His dedication, his attention to detail and his unique eye for talent, as both the manager of Manchester United and Aberdeen, has brought rich rewards. His CV is almost unique in a results-based profession that normally focuses on short-term solutions rather than long-term vision. He is a true visionary."

Michel Platini, three-time Ballon d'Or winner and current UEFA President.

"A person with such culture and intelligence can do any job he likes. I think his greatest achievement was to continue to change his teams and modernise them while continuing to win."

Marcello Lippi, World Cup-winning Italian manager.

"What a privilege to have played under arguably the best manager the world has ever seen. His record will surely never be eclipsed. It is simply astonishing to read through his managerial record of achievements."

Michael Owen, former Manchester United striker.

"Sir Alex, you were my idol for a coach, and you are an example for all future generations ... You are a legend and your achievements are unlikely to ever be surpassed."

Pelé, three-time World Cup winner.

"I will never forget the loyalty he showed me. Everything I have learnt I have learnt from the boss."

Ole Gunnar Solskjær, Champions League-winning striker.

"No one will be able to match his achievements, his dedication, his support for colleagues in need and his team-building know-how."

Roy Hodgson, England manager.

"Alex could eventually be the greatest manager ever. He is in that category of great managers for not only what he has achieved at Manchester United but what he started up at Aberdeen."

Denis Law, Manchester United legend.

"Whoever has gone to play for him, this winning mentality that he's got rubs off on you. People ask over the years what he's like and he's so driven and so determined and he works so hard at the job. When you finish and you hang up your boots it's no surprise that a few of us have gone into coaching. He sets such high standards that he's very difficult to follow. It's impossible to copy somebody like him."

Steve Bruce, former Manchester United defender.

"He made you feel passionate about the football club. He changed the mentality of every single individual. It's an incredible thing balancing the traditional aspects of life, his upbringing, with being open enough to move forward, to be modern and change with the modern game. He's the last of a kind. He was very simple in terms of his instruction but you knew full well you were playing at a football club that demanded performance."

Gary Neville, former Manchester United defender.

"Anybody who's been in his company and had the pleasure of working for him, you are struck by his passion, drive and desire to win football matches and trophies. That's just part of his DNA and you always sensed that being around him."

Mark Hughes, former Manchester United striker.

"The man is a magician. I can only say he'll be a big miss because he's simply the best."

Gianfranco Zola, former Chelsea player.

"I was one of the fortunate ones; I spent six fantastic years at Manchester United. I remember the first day I joined – I failed my medical and thought my move was going to collapse. But the way he treated me was like a son and I will never forget that."

Paul Ince, former Manchester United midfielder.

"You had to be a winner to be associated with him – from players, new players, everybody. If you didn't have that you wouldn't succeed with Sir Alex and he instilled that with everybody – from the top professionals to scouts watching B teams. His attention to detail was unbelievable."

Archie Knox, Ferguson's assistant at Aberdeen and Manchester United.

"He terrified us. I'd never been afraid of anyone before but he was such a frightening bastard from the start. Everything was focused towards his goals. Time didn't matter to him; he never wore a watch. If he wanted something done he'd stay as late as it took or come in early. He always joined in with us in training and would have us playing in the dark until his five-a-side team won. He was ferocious, elbowing and kicking."

Bobby McCulley, former East Stirlingshire forward.

"It has been a great honour and a pleasure to compete against Sir Alex."

Roberto Mancini, managerial rival at Manchester City.

"He is one of those people with an aura about him – you could just feel it. I think he's one of those great figures we see running through history; he's definitely got the gift of leadership."

Tony Fitzpatrick, former St Mirren captain.

"He's a leader of men. That's what he does best and it wouldn't have mattered where or when he managed a club like United, he would have been successful. His enormous mental strength is unquestionable."

Alex McLeish, former Aberdeen defender.

"Anyone would respect him because of what he has achieved. He brought a lot of young players through and it paid off and of course I have the utmost respect for him as a manager."

David Beckham, former Manchester United midfielder.

"He will be sorely missed by a lot of the managers in football because he would always speak to them, and he would always have a quiet word with anybody who was out of work or going into a job."

David Moyes, Ferguson's successor as Manchester United manager.

"We are all really lucky at Manchester United – really lucky – to have had twenty-five years of absolute paradise. Every season we are expecting to win something, and we usually do. And it's because of the manager, nobody else."

"He must certainly go down as the greatest manager in the history of the game. I would say more than that. In sport, in any sport, nobody has done more than he has done."

"I am a director at United but I hardly do anything because we are winning all the time and it is all down to Sir Alex Ferguson. He would get up in the middle of the night and travel three hundred miles if he thought there was a schoolboy he could sign. He loves the game."

Sir Bobby Charlton, Manchester United legend.

FERGUSON'S FAREWELL

On 12 May 2013 Sir Alex Ferguson gave a farewell speech to the crowd at Old Trafford following Manchester United's 2–1 victory over Swansea.

"I have no script in my mind. I'm just going to ramble on and get to the core of what this football club has meant to me.

First of all it's a thank you to Manchester United, not just the directors, not just the medical staff, the coaching staff, the players, the supporters, it's all of you. You have been the most fantastic experience of my life. Thank you.

I have been very fortunate. I've been able to manage some of the greatest players in the country, let alone Manchester United. All these players here today have represented the club the proper way. They won the championship in a fantastic fashion; well done to the players.

My retirement doesn't mean the end of my life with the club. I will now be able to enjoy watching them, rather than suffer with them. But if you think about it, those last-minute goals, the comebacks, even the defeats, are all part of this great football club of ours. It's been an unbelievable experience for all of us, so thank you for that.

I'd also like to remind you that when we had bad times here the club stood by me, all my staff stood by me, all the players stood by me. Your job now is to stand by our new manager. That is important.

Before I start blubbing, I just want to pay tribute to Paul Scholes, who retires today. He's unbelievable, one of the greatest players this club has ever had, and ever will have. Paul, we wish you a good retirement. I know you'll be around annoying me.

Also I'd just like to say a little word wishing Darren Fletcher a speedy comeback to our club.

I wish the players every success in the future; you know how good you are. You know the jersey you're wearing. You know what it means to everyone here, and don't ever let yourselves down. The expectation is always there.

Thank you from all the Ferguson family. Thank you, thank you."

On the timing of his retirement:

"[I wanted] to go out a winner. That is really important to this club. To go out a winner is the most important thing I ever wanted to do."

On the most important moment of his career:

"It's hard to look back. I've never done that. I think I've got plenty of time to do that now. I think the most important achievement, without doubt, was winning the first league. Once we won the first league the door opened, and we just grew and grew."

On what he will miss the most:

"Those last-minute goals. I love those last-minute goals."

Also available from Biteback

WE ATE ALL THE PIES

JOHN NICHOLSON

Football is weird. Damn weird. Why do we love it so intensely? Why are millions of us utterly obsessed by it? Is it a kind of drug or some sort of hypnosis? It can't just be the 22 preening millionaires running around on a rectangle of grass that keeps us all hooked. Have you watched football? A lot of it is so boring it can make your eyes melt.

In *We Ate All the Pies*, John Nicholson, gonzo sports writer and star columnist for www.football365.com asks a question which few, if any, have asked before: just why is football so damn popular? This is a unique, funny, warm and thought provoking excursion into our football lives, told in John's trademark off-beat, powerful and irreverent style.

Longlisted for the William Hill Sports Book of the Year award 2010

240pp paperback, £9.99
Available from all good bookshops or order from
www.bitebackpublishing.com